PRAYER

THE REAL BATTLE

© 2009 by Open Doors International
Published 2010 ISBN: 978-0-901644-11-4

Unless otherwise indicated, Scripture is taken from the HOLY BIBLE, NEW
INTERNATIONAL VERSION®. NIV®. Copyright © 1973, 1978, 1984 by
International Bible Society. Used by permission of Zondervan. All rights reserved.

Cover design by: Velvet Creative.
Printed in THE UNITED STATES OF AMERICA

PRAYER
THE REAL BATTLE

BROTHER ANDREW
AND AL JANSSEN

CONTENTS

1. Crisis

*The Book of Acts is filled with prayer meetings;
every forward thrust the first church made
was immersed in prayer. Take another look at
the church at Pentecost. They prayed ten days
and preached ten minutes and three thousand
people were saved. Today we pray ten minutes
and preach ten days and are ecstatic if
anyone is saved.*

RONALD DUNN

1. CRISIS

*Jesus never taught His disciples how to preach,
only how to pray. . . . To know how to speak to God
is more than knowing how to speak to man.*

ANDREW MURRAY

Several years ago a dear friend asked my colleague Al Janssen and me to undertake a highly confidential project. We were invited to intercede through prayer for twenty-two brothers in a Muslim region where there was no known indigenous church. During the previous four years, there had been a tremendous movement of God's Spirit, and several thousand people had come to believe in the Lord Jesus Christ as their Savior. These men and women were bravely witnessing for their Lord; several had already paid the price with their lives.

Because there was no visible church in this country, there were no institutions to support this work of the Spirit. There were no seminaries to train pastors. There were no experienced leaders who could nurture the new congregations that were forming nearly every week. There were no elders or deacons who might encourage those who were persecuted or support the widows whose husbands had died because of their witness for Christ. While there were a few foreign mission groups working in the area, most of them were humanitarian relief agencies that were not equipped to strengthen these infant churches.

> *God invites us to influence our community, our nation, and the world—to literally direct history while we're on our knees.*

My friend had identified twenty-two men, all Muslim followers of Jesus, who were potential pastors. For the next three years, they would meet secretly for one week each month, changing locations frequently, to receive intensive Bible and theological training. When their courses were successfully completed, they would be ordained as pastors to serve these congregations.

Of course, Al and I committed to pray for these men and recruited a few others to join us. What a privilege it was to go before our Lord and plead for the leaders of this church in a radical Islamic nation!

Within six months two of these brothers had died a martyr's death.

This precipitated a crisis in Al's life. Our assignment required far more than a simple "God bless these men" type of prayer. They needed committed intercessors—men and women who would plead on their behalf before God. They needed the protection of the body of Christ committed to fighting a spiritual battle on their behalf. This caused Al to pray, "Lord, You must teach me how to do this!"

I warned him, "This is the most dangerous prayer: 'Lord, make me a man of prayer.'"

Everywhere we go in the world, meeting with our brothers and sisters who suffer for the name of Christ, we hear the request, "Please pray for us." But how do we pray for them? Somehow we seem to know how to pray for our friends and family. Or do we really? As I listen to people pray in Holland or the United States or other free countries, it sounds like our prayers are mostly self-centered: "God, here's what I want."

It's fine to pray about our jobs and our children and our finances. Of course, we ask God to heal our sick neighbors and provide safe travel for loved ones. However, if that's all we do, we are missing out on a great adventure.

God invites us to influence our community, our nation, and the world—to literally direct history while we're on our knees.

That is what this booklet is about—to provide you with some practical lessons about prayer that we have learned from the Scriptures and from those who are persecuted for following Jesus. If we want to leave an indelible mark on the world, there is no more powerful way to do it than by joining in God's purposes through prayer. Our prayers can go where we cannot (although they are not a substitute for our going when we can). There are no borders, no prison walls, no doors that are closed when we pray. The political, economic, military, and spiritual leaders of the world may not know our names, but we can have more influence on their plans than all of their closest advisers put together. While many things may seem impossible from a human standpoint, in the realm of prayer there are no impossibilities.

Still we hesitate. A Christian man once told me, "It's not our place to tell God what we want Him to do with His world"—which is how he described intercessory prayer. "Why not?" I challenged him. God invites us—even commands us—to do it. Jesus said, "You may ask me for anything in my name, and I will do it" (John 14:14). Shall we decline His invitation out of false humility? God wants us to be active, not passive. He wants us to resist—and ultimately defeat—the principalities and powers that hold the world hostage. Further, He gives us weapons more powerful than theirs to do this. Jesus declares: "Whatever you bind on earth will be bound in heaven, and whatever you loose on earth will be loosed in heaven" (Matthew 16:19). God has given us access to the unlimited power of Jesus Christ—power far greater than that of any so-called "superpower" on earth.

Whenever our Lord prayed, things happened. No wonder the disciples asked Him to share the secret with them. "Lord, teach us to pray" (Luke 11:1), they said, even though they had been praying throughout their lives in their synagogues and homes. Prayer was the heart of Jesus' success.

> *God has given us access to the unlimited power of Jesus Christ—power far greater than that of any so-called "superpower" on earth.*

It is the key to our success in everything we do as Christians. It is the basis of everything God accomplishes. This is the reason we consider it so important for us to unlock these hidden reserves of divine power and confront the enemy who would sweep the earth with his evil plans.

Why don't you join us in attacking Satan's strongholds? This is the real battle that can change the course of history.

TAKE ACTION

On a scale from 0 to 10—with 0 meaning you never pray and 10 that you pray constantly for God's will to be done on earth as in heaven—how would you rate your prayer life today?

What one thing could you do this next week to move your prayer life one number closer to 10?

No man is greater than his prayer life....
The ministry of preaching is open to few;
but the ministry of prayer—the highest ministry
of all human offices—is open to everyone.

LEONARD RAVENHILL

2. WATCH AND PRAY

The meaning of prayer is that we get a hold of God, not of the answer.

OSWALD CHAMBERS

2. WATCH AND PRAY

*Prayer is not monologue but dialogue; God's voice
in response to mine is its most essential part.*

ANDREW MURRAY

The first time you visit a Muslim country,
the experience can be overwhelming. For
both of us, our first trip to Pakistan provided us
with sights and smells and cultural experiences
that were more than we could process. It took
time for us to adjust and to see what God was
doing in the lives of people in that nation.

More important than being aware of the
language and culture of a country is to discover
God's heart for people. This requires that we
go in with no program or agenda. We need to
start by listening to Him. Even though it seems
so natural for us to jump in and pray about
a situation as though we already know what
God needs to do, this kind of prayer is only a

one-way conversation in which we give God his marching orders.

In contrast, notice how Jesus prayed at every vital point in His ministry. The Gospel of Luke tells us that He prayed at His baptism. Note what happened: "As he was praying, heaven was opened and the Holy Spirit descended on him" (Luke 3:21-22). Jesus prayed when large crowds praised Him—He often withdrew to lonely places and prayed in order to gain necessary perspective and keep the right priorities (Luke 5:15). Jesus prayed all night when He decided on the twelve men who would be His inner circle (Luke 6:12-13). He prayed at the point when He revealed Himself to the disciples as the Messiah (Luke 9:18-22). He was praying when He was transfigured and talked with Moses and Elijah (Luke 9:28-29). He was praying when His disciples asked Him to teach them how to pray (Luke 11:1). And He prayed in the hour of our redemption.

Let's focus on this last situation—the account of Jesus' agony in the Garden of Gethsemane:

> *Jesus went out as usual to the Mount of Olives, and his disciples followed him. On reaching the place, he said to them, "Pray that you will not fall into temptation." He withdrew about a stone's throw beyond them, knelt down and prayed, "Father, if you are willing, take this cup from me; yet not my will, but yours be done."*

An angel from heaven appeared to him and strengthened him. And being in anguish, he prayed more earnestly, and his sweat was like drops of blood falling to the ground. When he rose from prayer and went back to the disciples, he found them asleep, exhausted from sorrow. "Why are you sleeping?" he asked them. "Get up and pray so that you will not fall into temptation." Luke 22:39–46

Victory must be won before the encounter with the enemy takes place. The climax in the life of Jesus was that moment on Calvary when He hung between heaven and earth,

> *Think of the opportunities we miss by not being awake, alert to God's work.*

separated from His Father as He bore our sins. But the real victory came in Gethsemane, when the decision to face the cross became final. That struggle in Gethsemane is described elsewhere: "During the days of Jesus' life on earth, he offered up prayers and petitions with loud cries and tears to the one who could save him from death, and he was heard because of his reverent submission. Although he was a son, he learned obedience from what he suffered" (Hebrews 5:7-8).

When Jesus prayed about a "cup" that might be taken from Him, I do not believe He meant the cross. Jesus was under such a crushing pressure in Gethsemane that He was literally at the point of death. Some uncertainty had entered into this "mission impossible." Whatever that uncertainty might have been, Jesus seemed to be actually dying in the garden under a burden that Satan had put on Him. But Jesus did not want to die in Gethsemane, because if He died there, He would not accomplish the redemption of the world. He could only do that on the cross.

> *Jesus…often withdrew to lonely places and prayed in order to gain necessary perspective and keep the right priorities.*

I don't think Jesus was praying for a way to avoid the cross. Thousands of martyrs, patriots, and others have died courageously because they thought they were dying for a worthy cause. Would Jesus back out? I don't believe that for a moment. Rather, the pressure of the devil had become so great as if to overwhelm Jesus completely. If the devil could kill Him in Gethsemane, then Satan would reign forever. Jesus wanted to go to the cross because God must reign forever and ever. The devil had to be defeated.

So the real victory occurred through prayer in Gethsemane. After this, there was no turning back, and there was no possibility of God diverting from the plan for the death of Jesus.

Too many of us pray when it's too late. Jesus said to the disciples in the garden, "Pray that you will not fall into temptation." We tend to pray after we have fallen into temptation. Jesus watched and prayed through His temptation, and so He was ready to go to Calvary. The disciples slept because of their sorrow, then wilted under the pressure, leaving Jesus alone, totally forsaken.

Prayer is the greatest way to thwart the devil's plans. Jesus teaches this precious lesson with His own deep, agonizing prayer. And "He was heard" (Hebrews 5:7). His prayers were granted; that cup of dying in Gethsemane was taken away; angels came and strengthened Him.

What a privilege for Peter, James, and John to be there with Jesus. Unfortunately, they made little use of that privilege. They slept! Of course, they had reasons to sleep—we will always find good excuses for our lapses. But then think of the opportunities we miss by not being awake, alert to God's work.

What were the disciples supposed to see? The suffering of their Lord. What are we to see today? The suffering and needs of this world— and the compassion God feels for those who are lost, like sheep without a shepherd. Oswald Chambers wrote: "'Tarry ye here, and watch with Me.' Is my idea of prayer based on the keen watching that Jesus Christ asked of His disciples?" Great question!

Learning to watch and pray was the first major lesson Al learned after crying out for God to teach him how to pray. Before every trip he began to pray: "Lord, may I see what you see, hear what you hear, love what you love, hate what you hate, and feel what you feel." This is a prayer God answers. He opens our eyes to gain glimpses of His heart—usually a glimpse at a time is all we can handle.

On one of our trips to the Middle East, God gave Al a look into the heart of a devout Muslim. We were eating dinner with a friend, a scholarly Muslim leader who has led several groups on the Hajj, the pilgrimage to Mecca that every Muslim is required to do at least once in his lifetime. We asked him to teach us what was required on the Hajj. Our friend explained all of the preparations before the trip: the pilgrim asks forgiveness of anyone he has offended, pays off all of his debts, and memorizes numerous verses from the Quran. He went on to describe the various ceremonies one does on the pilgrimage: everyone wears a white robe, circles the Kaaba, stones the devil, and offers an animal sacrifice.

At the end of his explanation, our friend said that a pilgrim must do all of these things precisely and with the right attitude or else the pilgrimage is a failure. If at any point the pilgrim slips in his devotion, he might as well stop there and head home—the Hajj is over for that person.

Knowing that millions of pilgrims are crowded together for five days, I said, "You mean if a man is jostled and gets angry, saying 'Get out of my way, you fool! ....'"

The professor sadly shook his head. "He has failed. The pilgrimage is over."

At that point Al says he felt for the first time deep compassion for Muslims who try so hard to please God by their efforts, but they have no comprehension of grace offered by a compassionate God through the sacrifice of Jesus Christ.

Without truth there can be no real compassion. That is why we must seek God, waiting and watching so we can see the world through His eyes. Whether dealing with personal or family issues, a community crisis, concerns for those who don't know our Lord, or national or international issues, this should be the starting point for our prayers. Without this perspective we will never become intercessors.

TAKE ACTION

Schedule one hour in the next week and spend it in a quiet place, with no agenda except to watch and pray. Write down what God says to you.

Martin Luther taught that if one were to be saying the Lord's Prayer, and a thought from God came into one's mind, it was necessary to stop praying and write it down, because what God says is more important than what we say.

SAINT FRANCIS DE SALES

3. Prepare For Battle!

*Most churches think their members are gathered
into one simply to take care of and build up each
other. They know not that God rules the world by
the prayers of His saints; that prayer is the power
by which Satan is conquered; that by prayer
the Church on earth has disposal of the powers
of the heavenly world.*

Andrew Murray

3. PREPARE FOR BATTLE!

Let's recognize something very important. God uses persecution for the good of the church. However, persecution is not the work of a loving God—it is the work of our sworn enemy.

Whenever we see evil, we can ask God to change that situation. We have every right to do so. But expect Satan to counter our efforts with every trick in his arsenal. He is an enemy of prayer, especially when we are asking God to free people from darkness and sin.

We all know the boundaries of evil are expanding every day, and fatalistic apathy enables those boundaries to grow because it offers no resistance. Christians must oppose evil. We are born for this battle! Every Christian is a soldier, a "member of God's resistance," engaged in spiritual warfare. The moment we lose sight of this, we become aimless in our actions and fuzzy in our focus. We forget why we were born and what we are trained and equipped to do on the battlefield, and we die without ever knowing why we lived. Most important, we never complete the mission we were sent to accomplish.

It's a fact that Christians live in enemy territory. Satan in the wilderness offered to give Jesus all the kingdoms of the world with their glory. Jesus didn't dispute that earth is under foreign occupation. The world is under Satan's control and his plan is to make sure everyone worships him. Our job is to return the world to its rightful owner—God. We are entrusted with the responsibility to advance God's Kingdom. The devil will do everything possible to thwart that goal.

Here are a few facts about the spiritual war:

- The church and the world are deadly enemies.

- It appears that evil has had success, but Christ will ultimately be victorious.

- God's hand, though unseen, is working.

- Prayer moves the unseen hand of God.

We as the body of Christ must join together

and take up arms against Satan. We have the authority to challenge his power with all the resources God has given us. In Ephesians Paul tells us to put on the full armor of God "so that you can take your stand against the devil's schemes" (Ephesians 6:11). So we buckle on the belt of truth, fasten the breastplate of righteousness, and for shoes put on the readiness to preach the gospel of peace. We hold up the shield of faith, put on the helmet of salvation, and grab the sword of the Spirit, which is the Word of God.

That's where we usually stop, dressed for battle, posing as though for a portrait. But that isn't where Paul ends his instruction. He continues: "pray in the

> *Christians must oppose evil. We are born for this battle!*

Spirit on all occasions" (v. 18). Now we're on the battlefield. Prayer is the battlefield! Fully armed, we persevere in our 'prayers for all Christians everywhere' (v. 18 NLT)."

Here Paul requests prayer for himself that he will boldly proclaim the mystery of the gospel (v. 19). This is a prayer all of us need. We need to pray for one another that we will be faithful in spreading the gospel in our communities and beyond. Our missionaries need us to pray for them to be bold in speaking the Good News of the kingdom. Our persecuted brothers and sisters need our prayers for faithfulness in loving and proclaiming Christ to their persecutors.

Does this really work? James writes: "Resist the devil, and he will flee from you" (James 4:7). We resist the devil through prayer.

> *Our job is to return the world to its rightful owner—God.*

At the first World Evangelism Congress in 1966 in Berlin, missionary Rachel Saint interviewed members of the Auca Indian tribe in Central America. These were vicious warriors who had killed her husband and four other missionaries who were trying to befriend them. But the love of Christ had transformed these men. After asking them to tell their stories, Rachel asked them what was their favorite Bible verse. The men conferred for a moment, then with a huge grin one of the men answered, "Devil, get out and never return!" That is a beautiful paraphrase of Jesus' words to a demon-possessed boy in Mark 9:25. Those warriors were right: we have the authority to order Satan and his minions to move off the scene so that the Kingdom of God may capture another section of enemy territory.

Never forget this fact: we share the love of God with people who are hostages of Satan in a world under his control. Prayer is the means by which we release the hostages.

TAKE ACTION

What evidence do you see of spiritual warfare in your life, in your family, in your community? What does this tell you about how to pray?

Consider how the war is impacting the lives of persecuted Christians around the world. How will this change the way you pray for them?

The battle for lost souls is won by prayer and intercession. Prayer is the warfare. Evangelism is not the attempt to win the battle—it is the mopping up operation. The physical possessions of the church, the buildings, organization and programs are the trucks we drive onto the field of battle to load up the spoils of the victory won by intercession.

RONALD DUNN

4. A New Time for Daily Prayer

To clasp the hands in prayer is the beginning of an uprising against the disorder of the world.

Karl Barth

4. A NEW TIME FOR DAILY PRAYER

Prayer is the act of seeing reality from God's point of view.

PHILIP YANCEY

In 1 Thessalonians 3:10 Paul says he is praying most earnestly day and night. How is it possible for Paul to work so hard in ministry while also praying constantly? This seems like an even greater challenge today with ever busier schedules and the constant access of email and cell phones. We can pray this way only if we recognize the unlimited opportunities we have. Every interruption is actually an opportunity to pray. An email can prompt you to pray for a friend. A phone call means you can ask a question and listen to see if there is a need in the person calling.

Also I find that watching the nightly news on television produces much prayer. In January 2009, over a three-week period, I watched the reports as Israel attempted to stop the rockets that Hamas was daily firing at their cities.

Now it is not my purpose to take sides in this conflict. But as I watched the reports, my first concern was, "How are our brothers and sisters faring?" I thought of a Christian doctor who works in Gaza's largest hospital. I wondered how he was dealing with the overwhelming influx of dead and injured Palestinians. I also thought of the widow of the Bible Book Shop manager, Rami—who was killed by Muslim fundamentalists in October 2007—how was she able in a war zone to care for three small children, including a baby who was born four months after her husband's death?

In that January attack, one of Israel's rockets hit Gaza's central police station where a ceremony was underway for the graduation of a new group of policemen. More than forty people were killed. Several bodies lay in the street outside the station—directly in front of Gaza Baptist Church.

Gaza is a small strip of land, only 30 miles long and 7 miles wide, containing 1.5 million people, nearly all of them Muslims. Serving the estimated 2,000 Christians is one small evangelical church in the heart of Gaza City.

Both Al and I have preached there and met with members to encourage them in their perilous situation, caught as they are between the forces of Hamas, Fatah, and the Israeli military.

We both thought about the many brothers and sisters with whom we had worshiped. Some of them had left Gaza after Rami was killed. The pastor and his wife were taking a sabbatical. Attendance at the church had fallen to a mere handful. Vibrant ministries that used to emanate from this church—Awana clubs, youth camps, leadership training for Palestinian

> *The course of an entire nation could be changed by one person saying to God, "What then will you do for your great name?"*

Authority officials, and much more—had ceased. Now this—how many more Christians would leave after the invasion was over? Would there be any church left? All of these thoughts caused us to pray—many times a day.

This is just one example of how the daily news can provide significant content for prayer. Of course, we believe in setting aside a dedicated quiet time—for us that is often early in the morning. But we also like to encourage friends to consider another dedicated time for prayer—when they read the newspaper or watch the news on television. The news provides an opportunity to practice Paul's admonition to "pray without ceasing."

As I watch the news, particularly the international news, there are two questions I always ask. First, "Is there a church?" Almost certainly a church exists in the region of the news report, even within the Islamic world. In many Muslim countries there has been a church for 2,000 years. Today that church may be weak but it still exists, shining a dim light in the darkness.

The second question is, "How will this news affect the church?" If the news is of an earthquake or tsunami or some other natural disaster, then our brothers and sisters are suffering along with the general population. If the news is political, it will affect Christians there, oftentimes negatively. If the news concerns a conflict, the church may be caught in the crossfire. In all cases these brothers and sisters need our prayers.

How many people prayed for the church in Iraq when the United States and coalition forces invaded the country to topple Saddam Hussein? We should have prayed, for that conflict has had devastating consequences. More than half of the estimated eight hundred thousand Christians living there have been displaced since the invasion. Muslim fanatics have burned churches, kidnapped Christians for exorbitant ransoms, and murdered them to steal their homes and businesses. Many received letters informing them that they had less than twenty-four hours to flee their homes, which were then taken over by Muslims. Christians have fled to Syria and Jordan or settled in refugee camps in the northern Kurdish region.

This is another example of how the current events in a country, which we may hear about on the news, affect our Christian brothers and sisters. While often we may not know the details, we can still pray for them. How can we do this? There is one prayer the church has used for 2,000 years: "Lord, have mercy." As we learn of turmoil and tragedy, we find ourselves breathing this prayer. "Lord, have mercy on those who are suffering. Lord, have mercy on our brothers and sisters who are affected by this event." With these words we acknowledge our helplessness and our need for God to intervene and use for good a situation that was probably intended for evil.

Another prayer we can use is drawn from the Lord's prayer: "Your will be done [in this situation] as it is in heaven." Again, we may not know what is specifically needed but we can ask that the Kingdom of God be made evident in that place.

Sometimes we find ourselves unable to say anything, yet we pray as Paul said in Romans: "The Spirit helps us in our weakness . . . the Spirit himself intercedes for us with groans that words cannot express." (Romans 8:26). In this way we identify with God and His creation that longs for wrong to be made right.

Both of us have been influenced by the example of Brother Lawrence, a seventeenth-century monk who said that the time of business does not differ from the time of prayer. "In the noise and clatter of my kitchen, while several persons are at the same time calling for different things, I possess God in as great tranquility as if I were upon my knees." In the same way, I observe the events of the world and remind myself God is in control. I can pray to Him about this situation by myself, in a prayer meeting, or while hearing the news reporter deliver the gory details.

> *Every interruption is actually an opportunity to pray.*

Another way of praying through the news is demonstrated by Joshua as the Israelites began to conquer the Promised Land. The fact that God had promised the land shows that the Lord had His mind set. Canaan was for Israel. Joshua was to lead them to victory. Predictably, there would be human problems, but the final result would be the same, because God had declared it.

During the first successful conquest at Jericho, Israel made a big blunder—they stole devoted things. As a result, thirty-six men died at Ai. Joshua cried out to God, and showed his experience as an intercessor when he made this statement: "What then will you do for your own great name?" (Joshua 7:9).

Do you understand what Joshua did? If he were here praying today, Joshua would ask God: "If the church of China is lost, or if those believers in Indonesia perish, or if the church in Gaza dies, then God, what are you going to do for your great name?" You can make the same plea: "God, for your glory in the world, for the sake of your great name, strengthen your church that suffers persecution."

You have no idea the tremendous influence you can have in the heavenlies and in world events if you become a true intercessor and pray through the news of our day. Wars could be stopped. The course of an entire nation could be changed by one person saying to God, "What then will you do for your great name?"

Once when I was in the hospital, a fruit basket was delivered to my bed with a get-well card and the text of Philippians 1:12: "What has happened to me has really served to advance the gospel." This is still God's primary concern. The gospel can be advanced no matter what the situation: inflation, unemployment, sickness, natural disasters, accidents. The apostle Peter called them "painful trials" (1 Peter 4:12). Such trials can destroy us or reveal gold. "When he has tested me, I will come forth as gold," Job said (Job 23:10).

This, then, should be our prayer—that the trials we experience or see others experiencing will further God's kingdom; that as his children suffer, going through the furnace of trials, we will come out as gold.

TAKE ACTION

Choose one of the following and do this at least once per week:

Read the local news in your daily or weekly newspaper and pray for individuals and situations that catch your attention.

Read the international section of your newspaper or a news magazine and pray for the church in the countries mentioned.

Plan to watch a national news show for half an hour and pray for the church in the countries mentioned.

If you are commuting to or from work, listen to an all-news station or news program for thirty minutes and pray for the church in the cities and countries mentioned.

*It is not a cowardly thing to pray; it is the only
way to get in touch with reality.*

OSWALD CHAMBERS

5. BECOME AN INTERCESSOR

*Intercession is not petition. Intercession is position.
It is not something we do—it is something we are.
It is not an exercise we engage in at a certain time
of the day—it is a life that we live.*

RONALD DUNN

5. BECOME AN INTERCESSOR

*By means of Intercessory Prayer God extends
to each of us a personalized, hand-engraved
invitation to become intimately involved in
laboring for the well-being of others.*

RICHARD J. FOSTER

D o you realize that Christianity is the only
religion in which you can disagree with
God? One of the clearest illustrations of this
kind of prayer is found in Exodus 32, where
God's own people, directly defying His express
command, have forsaken Him and turned to
idolatry. They pressured Aaron to "make us gods
who will go before us" (v. 1).

Understandably God is furious because they
are thwarting His ultimate plan and purpose
for Israel—to prepare the way for the coming

of their King. God is so angry that He says to Moses, "Now leave me alone so that my anger may burn against them and that I may destroy them" (v. 10). It appears obvious that God is finished with Israel. He is washing His hands of the people in whom He has invested so much.

> *If we are to see real change in our world, we must be willing to sacrifice.*

As we continue reading, we discover something unexpected. God holds out a carrot to Moses: "I will make you into a great nation" (v. 10). No man in history, apart from Abraham, ever had such an offer. I have to wonder if any of us standing before God would be able to turn down such a proposal. Amazingly Moses does not seize the honor. Instead, he pleads with God: "O Lord, why should your anger burn against your people, whom you brought out of Egypt with great power and a mighty hand? ... Turn from your fierce anger; relent and do not bring disaster on your people" (Exodus 32:11-12).

This is a classic picture of intercession. Oblivious to the world around him, Moses had only one consuming burden: I've got to get through to God. It's the only hope for my people, to somehow take away His anger. I must convince Him to change His mind! Moses is standing between God and Israel. This is a powerful demonstration of what one human being can do in prayer.

However, there is something more I want us to notice. A few years ago as I was re-reading Exodus 32, I saw something I'd never noticed before. In verse 11 the NIV translation says, "Moses sought the favor of the Lord his God." Unfortunately, that translation doesn't begin to hint at the intimacy between God and Moses. Eugene Peterson comes closer in *The Message* when he interpreted this verse: "Moses tried to calm his God down."

As I studied the Hebrew text, I discovered that the intimacy Moses had with God was much deeper even than that. If I were to translate the verse literally, it would read: "But Moses smoothed the wrinkles in the face of Jehovah."

This is astonishing! Moses was so close to a furious God that he could actually see Him and touch Him. Moses could see in God the deep wrinkles so common in the face of a very angry person. Then Moses had the audacity to reach out and touch that face.

What was it that burned in Moses' heart to keep him so close to an angry Deity? From our perspective it seems incredibly dangerous. If Moses wasn't careful, God just might wipe him out as well. But Moses knew his God. He was intimate with God. He did not "fear" God in the sense of being afraid of Him. In Exodus 33:11 it says that God would speak to Moses "face to face, as a man speaks with his friend." That is close!

Further, Moses truly loved his people. He cared for them so much that he was willing to die for them. Moses pleaded for God to forgive the sins of Israel. "But if not, then blot me out of the book you have written" (Exodus 32:32). Moses was offering to be a sacrifice for the people if it would mean their salvation. Of course, we know that God had another plan. Centuries later, Jesus would provide that substitutionary sacrifice.

In recent years we have determined that the most challenging aspect of prayer—real intercessory prayer—is being able to love with sacrificial compassion those for whom we pray. Often I have said that the classroom of prayer is located in the school of suffering. As my Queen Beatrix said in her televised Christmas address to the nation: "You see things differently through eyes that have wept." This is the challenge—to understand the needs of the people for whom we pray while simultaneously knowing the heart of God. Intercession joins both parts together

The apostle Paul understood this truth when he wrote in Romans 9:3 that he was willing to surrender his own salvation if only his Jewish brothers and sisters could be forgiven. There was no threat of rebellion in the prayers of Moses or Paul, only a deep love and willingness to suffer with Christ on behalf of sinful humans.

Just two things are needed for intercession:

close intimacy with God and a willingness to give one's life for those for whom we pray. If we are to see real change in our world, we must be willing to sacrifice. Yes, the atoning sacrifice of Jesus Christ was complete and sufficient to redeem all mankind, but He calls us to "Love one another. As I have loved you, so you must love one another" (John 13:34). Here's how to measure that: "Greater love has no one than this, that he lay down his life for his friends" (John 15:13).

The stakes are high. If we truly want our prayers, our intercession for loved ones near and far, to make a difference, then we must be willing to make the sacrifice. How important is this? What are you, what am I, willing to do? We may not be called to lay down our lives, but we are going to have to sacrifice. Are we willing to make the schedule changes necessary for intercessory prayer to be part of our daily routine? Are we willing to make the commitment to stay apprised of difficult situations around the world? Are we willing to accept the burden emotionally of bearing some of the suffering that our brothers and sisters around the world endure daily? And are we willing to persist in our prayers even when we

> *Just two things are needed for intercession: close intimacy with God and a willingness to give one's life for those for whom we pray.*

don't see, or aren't aware, of God's answers?

Those who are willing to adjust their lives to become intercessors are the people God will use to advance the Kingdom of Heaven around the world.

TAKE ACTION

If your church supports one or more missionaries, spend some time learning about them (perhaps through their newsletters) and praying for them, asking God to reveal to you how He would have you intercede.

Has God burdened you with a particular country where Christians are persecuted? Set aside a period of time to stand between these brothers and sisters and God.

To learn more about those countries in which persecution is most severe, see the World Watch List at www.opendoorsusa.org

The refusal to accept the harshness of God's ways in the name of his love was an authentic form of prayer. Indeed, the ancient prophets of Israel were not in the habit of consenting to God's harsh judgment and did not simply nod, saying, "Thy will be done." They often challenged him, as if to say, "Thy will be changed."

ABRAHAM JOSHUA HESCHEL

6. WIELD THE SWORD

Biblical prayer is impertinent, persistent, shameless, indecorous. It is more like haggling in an outdoor bazaar than the polite monologues of the church.

WALTER WINK

6. WIELD THE SWORD

How do we pray meaningfully for people we don't know very well? When we receive a prayer request in church or via email, we may know the need in general but have few if any details. It's even more challenging to pray for missionaries or persecuted Christians when often we have very little information about them. How do we pray specifically rather than superficially? An invaluable tool for prayer is the Word of God. This is the sword Paul wrote about in Ephesians 6, and we need to use it every day.

Wielding the Word of God, we literally can tell God what to do. Just as Moses challenged God, based on His promises to Abraham, Isaac, and Jacob (Exodus 32:13), so we can argue with God, based on His revealed promises.

Before you get too upset and tell me I just contradicted the message of chapter 2, let me show you what I mean. One of my dearest friends was Corrie ten Boom. Corrie was a passionate intercessor and her urgency and excitement were infectious. You couldn't pray with her without being changed by the experience.

> **Wielding the Word of God, we literally can tell God what to do.**

Many times in the midst of those lively prayer sessions, she would remind God of His promises. She would have made a terrific lawyer. She would grab her Bible and thumb through the pages rapidly until she found the exact passage to prove her case. Then she would lift her Bible into the air, point to the verse and say triumphantly in her strong Dutch accent, "Here, Lort—read it Yourself!"

I'm sure God loved that. He likes it when we know Him well enough to talk to Him that way. Corrie was not deterred by false piety or legalism or a need to be anyone but herself. Plus, as she would often remind Him, she was not asking God for anything He had not already promised. So she never hesitated to tell Him what to do and to thank Him when He did it. "I knew You would do it!" she would say. "I just knew it!"

You might wonder why, if God has made a promise, we need to pray and ask Him to fulfill it. I believe God's prophetic will, no matter how clearly set forth in Scripture, cannot happen until His conditions are met. One of those conditions concerns the prayers of His people. Take for example a clear promise about the exiles returning to Jerusalem: "This is what the Lord says: 'When seventy years are completed for Babylon, I will come to you and fulfill my gracious promise to bring you back to this place'" (Jeremiah 29:10). Seventy years! Clearly God's plans were fixed. Jeremiah had prophesied it. The time was set.

Nearly seventy years later, Daniel remembered this prophecy that God would take His people back to their land. At the time, it didn't look at all as though this could happen. Jerusalem was a heap of ruins and Israel was exiled to a faraway country. Daniel had served three successive governments in high positions. By this time he must have been ninety years old, perhaps no longer taking a decisive leadership role. But when he realized the implications of the prophecy, he reacted as an intercessor. "So I turned to the Lord God," Daniel writes, "and pleaded with him in prayer and petition, in fasting, and in sackcloth and ashes" (Daniel 9:3).

One requirement for an intercessor is to give undivided attention to the Lord. You cannot allow your plans or your interests or even your problems to receive primary attention. You must concentrate only on the God you serve. Daniel, who had lived like a prince in the palace of the king, was so intent in this task that he stripped off his beautiful clothing and put on sackcloth as he prayed and fasted. That sounds a bit overboard. Why such "fanaticism"? After all, God had spoken—this was a sure thing. So what is Daniel's concern? Why is he so terribly upset about the matter?

Here's the point: God still needed a man to do what He said had to be done between the prophecy and its fulfillment. A time of repentance and intercession was required. God's prophetic will, no matter how clearly set forth in Scripture, cannot happen until His conditions are met. While Daniel prayed, confessing his sin and the sins of his people and "making my request to the Lord my God for his holy hill" (v. 20), the angel Gabriel came to him with a message. God's messenger explained that "Seventy 'sevens' are decreed for your people and your holy city to finish transgression, to put an end to sin, to atone for wickedness, to bring in everlasting righteousness, to seal up vision and prophecy and to anoint the most holy" (v. 24). Gabriel gives Daniel, and us, the big picture. The Israelites would return to Jerusalem as promised, but the story wouldn't be over. Daniel, by praying as he did, received more than his request. He learned about the coming Messiah who would put an end to sin.

An invaluable scriptural weapon for intercession is the Psalms. When we don't know what to pray, these ancient prayers and

hymns help us express our yearnings for God
to thwart the plans of an evil world. "O God,
the nations have invaded your inheritance,"
writes Asaph in Psalm 79. Frequently I feel
this way about what is happening to the church
around the world. Then I pray with the psalmist:
"Help your people who are persecuted, O God
our Savior, for the glory of your name; deliver
them and forgive their sins for your name's
sake. Why should the nations say, 'Where is
their God?' . . . May the
groans of my brothers
and sisters who are in
prison come before
you; by the strength
of your arm preserve
those condemned to
die" (paraphrased from
Psalm 79:9-11).

> *God's prophetic
> will, no matter how
> clearly set forth in
> Scripture, cannot
> happen until His
> conditions are met.*

Al has a habit of praying one or more psalms
daily for the twenty brothers we mentioned in
chapter 1 who are training for ministry. "In you,
O Lord, I have taken refuge," says David in
Psalm 31. Al uses this to pray, "Lord, may my
brothers take refuge in you today." Later in this
Psalm David talks about his distress: "My eyes
grow weak with sorrow, my soul and my body
with grief. . . . Because of all my enemies, I am
the utter contempt of my neighbors" (Psalm
31:9, 11). Clearly this is often the situation of
our brothers. As Muslim followers of Jesus,
they are despised by many of their family and
community. Is it too much to imagine that

their eyes grow weak with sorrow? Many of the psalms have similar sentiments, which we can apply as prayers for people we know today. We can pray the psalms for ourselves, for close friends and relatives, and for those far away whose circumstances are not so clear.

One more thing: sometimes God will plant in your mind the need to encourage someone specifically with Scripture you have read or prayed. There is a brother in the Muslim world for whom both of us intercede on a daily basis. Recently this man instituted a bold, new initiative that would place Bibles into Islamic institutions. Several of these schools were grateful—they wanted to go to primary sources to learn what Christians believe, no doubt to be better able to witness about Islam against Christianity. But some of the institutions were angry about this offer. Threats were made against our brother.

One morning Al was reading in Exodus 5 and 6. God had ordered Moses to go to Egypt and speak to Pharaoh demanding that he free the Israelites. Pharaoh's initial response to the message was anger and an increase in the cruel workload of the Israelites, who then complained to Moses. Rather than freeing them, Moses' message had made their situation worse. The ten plagues and the many miracles God performed were yet to come. Al sensed that this was the situation for our friend. Initially when we obey God's direction, our efforts may seem to make a situation worse. Later we begin to see God's hand. After praying for our friend, Al dropped him a short email, reminding him about this passage and how it had prompted him to pray and encouraging our brother to persevere through the trial.

It doesn't take long to write a one-or two-sentence note of encouragement. This is another way an intercessor can minister—by occasionally telling the person how you are praying for him or her.

TAKE ACTION

For the next week, pray a psalm each day on behalf of someone for whom you are interceding. On one of those days, write a short note of encouragement to this person to tell him or her how you are praying.

Psalms offers a helpful pattern of expressing rage that the Church often tries to repress. . . At a basic level, the psalms help me reconcile what I believe about life with what I actually encounter in life. . . . [Psalms] contains the anguished journals of people who want to believe in a loving, gracious, faithful God while the world keeps falling apart around them.

PHILIP YANCEY

7. PRAY WITH,
NOT JUST FOR

*Who can say what power a church could develop
and exercise, if it gave itself to the work of prayer
day and night for the coming of the kingdom, for
God's power on His servants and His word, for the
glorifying of God in the salvation of souls?*

ANDREW MURRAY

7. PRAY WITH, NOT JUST FOR

A few years ago Al attended a large prayer meeting in Cairo. Each Monday at one of the main Protestant churches in the city, more than eight hundred people, mostly young adults, gather in the evening for three hours of prayer. Apart from a brief ten-minute meditation by the leader, they spend the time worshiping and praying for their country. Their primary request is for the nation to come to Christ. They are praying that millions of Muslims in Egypt will meet Jesus. This isn't the only prayer meeting in Egypt—there are many like it all over the country.

In the course of the service, one of the participants read loudly from the prophet Isaiah: "So the Lord will make himself known to the Egyptians, and in that day they will acknowledge the Lord. They will worship with sacrifices and grain offerings; they will make vows to the Lord and keep them" (Isaiah 19:21). That sparked several to claim the verse and other promises about Egypt in Isaiah. Passionately they poured out their hearts: "God come and heal Egypt as you promised!"

Later Al had a conversation with the pastor who helped organize these meetings. Because of an attempt on his life, we cannot name him. Based on the promises of Isaiah 19, this pastor said, "We're praying for a real awakening. We believe God wants to pour out His Holy Spirit over this nation." He was seeing evidence that God was answering those prayers. "We need to love Muslims and see them loved by Christ. A few years ago I didn't observe that. But lately I've started to see Christians praying for Muslims. We pray especially for visions and dreams and we see answers every day. Christ is revealing Himself in visions and dreams. We see Muslims coming to us, asking us questions because of the visions."

> *Our persistence (in prayer) means we have no other solution.*

In the course of the discussion, Al asked how Western Christians could pray for their brothers and sisters in Egypt. The pastor responded by saying, "Please don't pray for us. Please pray with us." Al asked for an explanation. "If you pray for us, you will pray for the wrong things," the pastor said. "You will pray that the church will be safe. You will pray for persecution to cease. We are not praying for these things. We ask God for the salvation of Egypt. We ask that He draw millions of Muslims to Christ. We ask that we will be bold and clear in sharing our faith with Muslims. And we pray that when the inevitable persecution comes—and there will be a major backlash from fundamentalists when many Muslims turn to Christ—that we will not run away, that we will be faithful in that persecution even if it costs us our lives. Will you tell your friends to pray these prayers with us?"

For many Christians this is a new way of praying.

The pastor also exhorted his congregation and us in the West to keep on praying. Referring to the parable of the persistent widow in Luke 18, he said, "Jesus showed His disciples that they should always pray and not give up. Why are we coming together on Monday evenings? Our persistence means we have no other solution. Our persistence means we love our friends, and we will keep on begging for our friends—for the people of this country and the whole Arab world. God says through the prophet Isaiah, 'I will gather all nations and tongues, and they will come and see my glory.' Do we believe that? Let us take big prayers to the Lord. Let us be bold."

This attitude is not unique to Egypt. Al and his wife, Jo, had another experience when they met with three of the brothers mentioned in Chapter 1. These three who risked their lives daily to serve Christ were asked how we could pray for them. Here were their requests: for boldness in sharing their faith, for continued growth of the church—all of the believers in this area are converts from Islam—and for translation of needed resources so the church can grow. As Al and Jo left that meeting, they were struck by the unselfishness of these prayer requests. These brothers didn't even ask prayer for safety—in fact one of them had recently been badly beaten.

This is the heart of the persecuted church: that the gospel will advance. Let's pray with them, for we know this desire matches the heart of God. The apostle Peter tells us that God is not slow in keeping His promise, at least not as we understand slowness. "He is patient . . . not wanting anyone to perish, but everyone to come to repentance" (2 Peter 3:9).

Of course, not everyone can meet these dear believers in person and learn their requests as we have. This is the reason each month Open Doors publishes requests from the persecuted church so you can know their hearts. Here are a few recent requests from believers in various countries:

- **Bangladesh:** for distribution of Bibles among rural churches.

- **Bhutan:** believers are hungry for solid discipleship and biblical training.

- **An Asian country:** pray for six scholars in theological studies preparing to enter Muslim ministry on graduation.

- **Kenya:** pray for church leaders and members in an area of conflict to have boldness to share the gospel with local Muslims.

- **India:** for strengthening of the Christian community in Orissa where violence has left thousands shattered.

- **Arabian Peninsula:** that biblical movies from the Internet will be seen by many young people who own mobile phones and are seeking the truth.

- **Iran:** for distribution of Christian literature inside the country.

- **Iraq:** in Mosul that various sections of the population will live in harmony, and that the Christians will learn to forgive the perpetrators of violence against them.

- **Israel:** for reconciliation efforts between Palestinian Christians and Messianic Jews.

- **China:** for the discipleship of new congregations formed after the massive earthquake in Sichuan.

TAKE ACTION

The list above represents only a few of many prayer requests we receive from around the world each month. As you read them, ask God to show you the heart of the people behind these situations. Then join with them in prayer for the advancement of the Kingdom of God.

Intercession leaves you neither time nor inclination to pray for your own "sad sweet self." The thought of yourself is not kept out, because it is not there to keep out; you are completely and entirely identified with God's interests in other lives.

Oswald Chambers

8. A Vital Question

It is not so true that "Prayer changes things" as that prayer changes me, and then I change things; consequently we must not ask God to do what He has created us to do.

Oswald Chambers

8. A VITAL QUESTION

*The world can beat the Church at everything
—except this: living out the life of Christ.*

RONALD DUNN

As we saw in chapter 4, we are called to pray constantly. But if you decide to do this, you should understand that it's hard work. Further, it is dangerous to be an intercessor. We say this not to discourage you but rather to warn you. Al began praying for the persecuted church in the mid–1990s and it soon became part of his daily prayer routine. Then something happened. Prayer was no longer enough—he had to do something. In fact he was compelled to get involved. His wife sensed it too and suggested that they downsize their home and simplify their lives so that they were prepared for whatever God wanted them to do. Some of their friends didn't understand why they would move

out of their dream house into a smaller home—
that's the opposite of the American dream.

In 2001, shortly after the events of
September 11, Al joined hands with me to go to
the persecuted church in the Muslim world. The
result was numerous opportunities to minister
to individuals, to preach and teach in various
churches, and to write two books. This leads us
to ask the following question: Are you willing to
become part of the answer to your prayers?

We must not substitute prayer for obedience.
Whenever we pray for family or friends or
our community or for certain countries or the
persecuted church, we must realize that God
may call us to do more. To hear God's call to us,
we need to know about a need. We should obey
the Scriptures where Jesus instructed us in John
4:35 to open our eyes up and look at the fields.
In other words, get acquainted with the vastness
of the need.

Too many Christians say, "God never called
me." But I would say that they have never
listened to the call—because God has called
you. He has told you to get acquainted with the
needs in the world. We may complain about the
modern news media that dump all the problems
of the world into our living room. Actually, they
leave us without a single excuse for saying that
we do not know about the need.

One of my favorite books of the Bible is

Nehemiah. His name means "comfort given by Jehovah," and indeed, he lived that out. Nehemiah had a prestigious job as cupbearer to the Persian King Artaxerxes. He lived a comfortable life but he never forgot his roots. So when several brothers saw him after visiting Judah, Nehemiah questioned them about the Jewish remnant and the condition of the city of Jerusalem.

When Nehemiah questioned his brethren, he heard this shattering report: "Those who survived the exile . . . are in great trouble and disgrace. The wall of Jerusalem is broken down, and its gates have been burned with fire" (Nehemiah 1:3). What a terrible picture they painted! But they had clearly stated the need. I believe in his heart Nehemiah was willing to react to whatever the answer might be. In other words, he was willing to share their problems, to sit down, to listen and pray and help.

> *Too many Christians say, "God never called me." But I would say that they have never listened to the call.*

This is the moral obligation we have before we dare ask how anybody is doing. We must be willing to listen and pray and help. If our attitude is not the same as that of Nehemiah, then God will not use us. So my question is, "Do you really want to know about the condition of your brothers and sisters around the world?" Because if you want to know, you can know.

When Nehemiah heard about the tremendous need of his brethren, he reacted strongly: "When I heard these things, I sat down and wept. For some days I mourned and fasted and prayed before the God of heaven" (v. 4). I'm not suggesting that we should weep too much in public. But I think that if we really wish to identify with the needs of suffering brothers and sisters, even though we may never have met them, the gift of tears is necessary. Our tears will drive us to pray, and we may even fast.

After a time of prayer, there comes another question: Is there something I can do? In essence, Nehemiah said to God: "Here I am." Now this presented a potential problem. If he decided to go back to Judah, he would have to give up a very good, secure position and launch out into the unknown. First, he would have to speak to the king, and in those days that was a dangerous thing to do. Even to be sad in the presence of the monarch was punishable by death. Still Nehemiah knew something had to change in Jerusalem, just as you and I know that something has to change in the world today. It is my earnest conviction that God has given to His children all the resources to meet the needs of the world. But no change will come the easy way; we will have to pay a price.

The day came when Nehemiah returned to work, and the king asked him, "Why does your face look so sad when you are not ill? This can be nothing but sadness of heart" (2:2). In the text Nehemiah admits that he was very afraid. This was a crucial moment in his life. He didn't deny his emotions but briefly stated the problem. Then the king said to him, "What is it you want?" (v. 4).

I'm not sure Nehemiah expected this but clearly he had thought about what he needed to do. The next verses say simply: "Then I prayed to the God of heaven, and I answered the king, 'If it pleases the king and if your servant has found favor in his sight, let him send me to the city in Judah where my fathers are buried so that I can rebuild it.'"

In Nehemiah we find an exceptional man doing a secular job. But God wanted him to do a special work for his nation, Israel, something that not everybody could do. This is the case today. God calls people out of the world who are doing something anybody can do, because he wants them to do a job that only they can do. Every Christian should ask, "Lord, what do you want me to do?" If we ask God, He will give us an answer. And if

> *If each Christian does what God wants him or her to do, we will have a total spiritual revolution in our churches.*

each Christian does what God wants him or her to do, we will have a total spiritual revolution in our churches, because God has a job for each one of us, a job that no one else can do.

> ***This is the heart of the persecuted church: that the gospel will advance.***

Just how far are we willing to go in obeying God's call? How much of our comfort and pleasure and "security" are we willing to sacrifice, if necessary, so that others may live? How much opposition are we willing to face? We may sing that we have laid "our all on the altar"—but are we ready to lay down our possessions, our careers, our plans for a quiet, comfortable retirement, maybe even our lives? Are we willing to go where God tells us to go—even places where we might be imprisoned, tortured, or killed for sharing the gospel? Are we, in fact, prepared to face the disapproval or ridicule of neighbors, colleagues, family, or other Christians as we take a bold stand for God? If we are going to battle Satan with any real effectiveness, I am convinced that we must confront these questions.

The Lord has exciting plans and He wants nothing more than to involve us in His plans. He has battles for us to fight, mountains for us to climb, exploits for us to perform. He waits for us to respond to this call of Jesus: "Follow me." Our task is the same as that of Jesus when

He ministered on earth: to share the love of God with people who are hostages of Satan in a world under his control.

To be sure, we cannot hope to carry any of this out by our own power or with our own authority. God must authorize and empower us every step of the way. That is why we always return to the battlefield of prayer.

It is my hope that through these short chapters you have gained some insight into how God wants to use you to influence our world. We are not helpless bystanders but fully equipped warriors ready to step into the fray and influence the advancement of God's Kingdom.

So will you strap on your armor? Will you watch and pray to discover God's heart for His creation? Will you watch the news and pray for your brothers and sisters who are affected by world events? Will you pursue an intimacy with God so close that you can truly intercede for your brothers and sisters around the world? Will you use your Bible as a weapon, a sword to claim the promises of God for those who suffer? Finally, will you learn the needs of your fellow believers and pray with them, not just for them?

Be careful. If you do all these things, God may ask you to become part of the answer to your prayers. If that happens, rejoice, for then you will be participating in the greatest adventure imaginable!

TAKE ACTION

Review the "Take Action" sections in this booklet. What is God saying to you about your prayer life now? What one change will you make in your prayer life from this point forward? Write it down and put it in your daily planner.

What would happen if we followed literally Jesus' command to love our enemies and pray for those who persecute us? How would it affect the reputation of Christians in the United States if we became known not for our access to the White House but for our access to heaven on behalf of those who strenuously, even violently, disagree with us?

PHILIP YANCEY

SOURCES

Quotes by Ronald Dunn from *Don't Just Stand There, Pray Something* (Thomas Nelson Publishers, 1992).

Quotes by Andrew Murray from *With Christ in the School of Prayer* (Revell, 1953).

Quote by Leonard Ravenhill from the article "The Passion of Prayer" (source unknown).

Quotes by Oswald Chambers taken from *My Utmost for His Highest* and *If Ye Shall Ask*, see *The Complete Works of Oswald Chambers* (Discovery House Publishers, 2000).

Quote by Saint Francis de Sales, 1567–1622, source unknown.

Quotes by Karl Barth and Richard J. Foster from *Prayer: Finding the Heart's True Home* by Richard J. Foster (HarperOne, 1992).

Quote by Brother Lawrence from *The Practice of the Presence of God*, translated by Donald Attwater (Templegate, 1974)

Quotes by Abraham Joshua Heschel, Walter Wink, and Philip Yancey from *Prayer: Does It Make Any Difference?* by Philip Yancey (Hodder and Stoughton, 2006); and from *The Bible Jesus Read* by Philip Yancey (Zondervan, 1999).

Some thoughts in chapters 5 and 6 are developed in more detail in *And God Changed His Mind* by Brother Andrew with Susan DeVore Williams (Chosen Books, 1990).

Some thoughts in chapters 7 and 8 were developed in greater detail in *Secret Believers* by Brother Andrew and Al Janssen (Revell, 2007).

:he *ministry* of Open Doors...
your link to the persecuted church

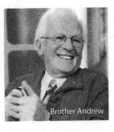
Brother Andrew

Open Doors was founded in 1955 by a young Dutchman named Brother Andrew to encourage Christians who were suffering behind the communist Iron Curtain. Driving a small Volkswagen Bug, Brother Andrew smuggled shipments of Bibles and other literature across closed borders, earning him the nickname of "God's Smuggler."

Today, Open Doors helps strengthen the faith of persecuted Christians in 60 countries across Africa, East Asia, Latin America and the Muslim world.

Open Doors **USA**
PO Box 27001
Santa Ana, CA 92799
USA

+1 949 752 6600
www.opendoorsusa.org

Open Doors
Serving persecuted **Christians** worldwide

LIGHT FORCE

A Stirring Account of the Church Caught in the Middle East Crossfire
Brother Andrew and Al Janssen

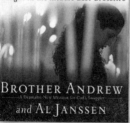

"This is a book that invites applause and criticism. It will edify and offend, fostering healthy and much-needed discussion and debate in the Western Church."

– Randy Alcorn, author, Safely Home

For years, Christians have fle from the horrific conflict in th Middle East. Today, in the la where the church began, less than two percent of the peop in Israel, West Bank, and Gaz are Christians. Yet that remna holds the hope for peace—if they can only persevere in fai and not be discouraged.

Light Force is the remarkable story of Brother Andrew's miss to seek out the church in the Middle East, learn about its conditions and needs, and do whatever he can to strengthen what remains. Through drama true stories, readers get an exclusive behind-the-scenes lo at real people affected by the centuries-old conflicts in this volatile part of the world.

This gripping account of the church caught in the crossfire v captivate readers everywhere.

Available from:

Open Doors
Serving persecuted Christians worldwide

Open Doors USA
PO Box 27001
Santa Ana, CA 92799 USA
www.opendoorsusa.org

SECRET BELIEVERS

WHAT HAPPENS WHEN MUSLIMS TURN TO CHRIST?

Brother Andrew and Al Janssen

his most incredible and eye-opening book to date, Brother
ndrew invites you to meet brave men and women you never
new existed.

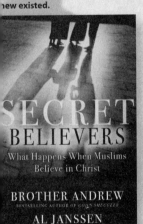

This is the riveting true story of the church in Islamic countries struggling to come to grips with hostile governments, terrorist acts, and an influx of Muslims coming to Christ. The names and places have been changed to protect the real people in real places. But the stories are true.

Secret Believers not only gives you a glimpse of the lives of these courageous believers, it also proposes four practical initiatives for Christians in the West to help these persecuted brothers and sisters. It calls us to join a new kind of jihad, leaving vengeance behind in favor of forgiveness, radical love, and unyielding prayer.

"Brother Andrew and Al Janssen reveal the amazing stories of those who witness the love of One they once refused and passionately searched until they found Him, even in the face of great opposition. Theirs is a testament to meekness, grace, and triumph, and a call to every follower of Christ to mirror their example."

– Ravi Zacharias, author and speaker

Available from:

Open Doors USA
PO Box 27001
Santa Ana, CA 92799 USA
www.opendoorsusa.org